Fully Booked Retreats

Your Guide for Explosive Business Growth

NATASA DENMAN

First published by Ultimate World Publishing 2018
Copyright © 2018 Natasa Denman
ISBN: 978-1-925884-00-5

Cover design: Ultimate World Publishing
Layout and typesetting: Ultimate World Publishing
Editor: Anita Saunders

ULTIMATE WORLD
— PUBLISHING —

Ultimate World Publishing
Diamond Creek,
Victoria Australia 3089
www.writeabook.com.au

Throughout this book you will find a number of underlined words that lead to resources which will help you with what you are learning. The easiest way to get access to these is via the ebook version which has these words hyperlinked. Email natasa@natasadenman.com with the subject line 'Retreat Ebook' and I will send it to you for free.

Dedication

I dedicate this book to the courageous first-time authors that put their trust in us to write their first books through the Ultimate 48 Hour Author retreat program. They took the leap of faith and embarked on a transformational journey. Our time with each and every one of you will forever be etched in our memories.

FREE Bonus Training

Want to run High-End Retreats to:

- stop selling your time for money
- work one-on-one
- be able to scale your business to multiple six and seven figures
- create transformation instead of just sharing information
  ... and have a ton of fun along the way?

Well, the very first step is to write a book which will be the system and backbone for your retreat program. Without a system, you have no compelling offer to sell as a high-end program.

Register for this FREE Training that will show you exactly how to write a book in just 48 Hours (limited time offer): "The Ultimate 48 Hour Author Blueprint that has helped over 300 first-time authors complete their books in a weekend".

If you still have fear around writing your first book, go and grab a copy of _Shut Up and Write Your First Book_. There is also a Free Bonus in there for you to read about the journeys of over 30 first-time authors.

Contents

Chapter 5

Chapter 6

Chapter 7

Introduction

People who don't pay, they don't pay attention, people who pay little, pay little attention and people who pay a lot, they pay a lot of attention — Unknown.

I never started out on a journey to run high-end transformational retreats. My inner desire was to change how people got results after investing into high-end educational programs to improve their lives or businesses. The reality that only 3% of people actually follow through when having invested in mentors, programs or seminars was too hard to swallow and not rewarding enough.

I had achieved the goal of having a fully booked coaching practice. I had licensed intellectual property that sold like hot cakes and experienced the sad but true reality that now many of my clients would never go on to create the transformation they sought or build the amazing business they set out to design their ultimate lifestyle.

I wanted to find a way that people would commit and stick to a process that would guarantee a successful personal and business transformation. That is why I tried out the model of running high-end retreats—to ensure that people in a situation where they are away from distractions, fully focused and fully committed financially and emotionally would do what they set out to do, no excuses!!!

Thus, the Ultimate 48 Hour Author retreats were born. They were born as a way to 'trick' first-time authors into actually following through and completing their first books. My journey into the world of mentors, programs and seminars has been a very successful one. When I commit and have skin in the game to someone or something, I am very disciplined to do the work and get massive Return on Investment for what I signed up to do. I realised very quickly not everyone is like that.

I was diploma number 109 out of 9000 students that had enrolled into the school I studied as a coach. I saw first-hand that when people invested in my licensed intellectual property of Ultimate Weight Loss – Lose the Last 10 Kilos not many followed through and got the results I did. There was a serious problem here—was it me or the mindset of the individuals involved? I quickly learned that it was mindset at the forefront of everything. So how do you make people follow through? The old saying 'You can lead a horse to water, but you can't make it drink' is an easy opt-out of taking responsibility.

I found the cure to procrastination and I bet you are dying to know what it is. It's so simple really. *Make a commitment to someone else.* This became my first trick to having my Ultimate 48 Hour Authors follow through on their commitment to the program. I started making them pre-sell their unwritten books to their warm networks and community. This was a massive move. We would create a 3D mock-up cover for them in time for their retreat and they would create a ready PayPal button link that they would share on their social, email and private networks on the first night of their retreats. Wow!!! Super scary for all these authors-to-be—actually announcing that they were writing a book and asking to be paid for it at a special pre-release price three to four months before the book's release date. Nevertheless, this action got everyone into action. It got everyone to feel amazing about the support they started to receive and solidified the decision they made when they chose to go on this journey. To this day I just love seeing and hearing the squeals that come from our authors when someone has bought their book and that people actually care and are full of support rather than criticism.

The second 'trick' I decided to instil into my high-end retreat program was the fact that when they work with us they get full end-to-end help with writing their book. I chose to take 100% responsibility to help my authors in pulling together this massive and overwhelming project of writing their first book. This would require managing and fulfilling other roles I was not an expert in, like editing, layout, design, transcription and publishing savvy. I had to bring in the experts to make this a full, all-inclusive experience and program that would turn the offer into a NO-BRAINER.

Thus, I chose to write this book—my ninth title and the solution to the question I have been asked lately: 'Nat, how do you run these amazing retreats four to six times a year and continuously fill them with high-quality clients that enable you to live your ultimate lifestyle?' The answer to that question lies in the statement: *If you are willing to do what I've done and consistently do, then you can have what I have.*

What do I actually mean by that? So many watch my journey on social media (you are welcome to join in—just look me up under Natasa Denman and follow me) and say 'I want to do what you are doing'. However, the reality of social media is that we all portray the best of ourselves and our businesses. No one wants to watch or follow a sourpuss or a whinger. What most of you don't see are the moments of rejection I get, the amount of travel I do to find my authors, the times when I feel like my business is imploding and the fear I sometimes have that things won't work out. I feel guilty as any parent (you can read all about that in the *Guilt Free Parents* book my husband and I wrote) when I need to be away from my children, at times for two to four weeks, to sustain this type of business.

I absolutely love what I do. It is all worth it. I change people's lives, I transform insecure personalities to confident and certain individuals and businesses, I have a library of my own authors that are changing the world to make it a better place. I am contributing on a massive scale. I am addicted to my purpose. My clients are a delight to serve and they form part of a bigger family I am part of. No sane person would do what I do. You have to be a bit nuts and super disciplined to follow this path. You need to be obsessed!

If you are a person that wants to change the individual or business owner through running high-end transformational retreats then keep reading—you will have all the tools in your hands to do exactly that. It won't be easy—but I can guarantee it will be worth it. It will require more work than you ever anticipated but it will give you more fulfilment than you ever imagined.

Use this book as a guide and shortcut to avoid the mistakes I made over my time in running high-end retreats. Don't try to cut corners, and always improve on how and what you do at your retreats. This is not a journey for the faint-hearted, but for those that aspire to be a leader and transformative facilitator of change.

I like to give my students a ton of 'how to'; I don't fluff around. I like to share what works and what doesn't from the basis of my personal experience. I can never teach anything I haven't done myself. After having run over 20 high-end retreats and mastering a formula that works, I will be teaching you the exact steps I followed and still follow to continue filling my client base with amazing individuals.

Aim to give your clients a once-in-a-lifetime, unforgettable experience that they will treasure forever. Be authentic, real and serve from a heart space. Take the responsibility that most will never dare to take. You are a Change Maker—Own it, Live it, Breathe it. It's your turn now …

Chapter 1
Your Magnetic Retreat Offer

So you want to help people? You know what they need. Maybe they are hurting or they are stuck in life or their business/career? You have an amazing idea for a retreat—a place where you can take them away from their worries and busy life, and help them solve a problem through an amazing experience. Great! The only problem is, people don't buy what they need—they buy what they WANT!

The biggest mistake I have seen in the space where experts want to run retreats is that they try to sell FLUFF: Be empowered, connect with your feminine power, self-care, heal your wounds. I am sorry, but that says nothing at all. Those are also all needs to a bigger problem that is keeping your ideal client awake at night. Your client's deep desire is more superficial and ego-driven. Your client still doesn't know what they don't know. It is your job to communicate and evolve their thinking to a point that they believe 100% you are the person to help them solve the problem.

We all wish we had a magic wand we could wave and make certain things happen or disappear. That magic wand is our ego at play. What does it want? A magic bullet, of course. The ego buys so that the soul can receive.

Here is an example: The first niche I ran a coaching

practice under was weight loss. For my clients to be successful they needed to plan, set goals, get organised, understand nutrition and movement, and work on their mindset. What they wanted was quite different. They wanted to lose five kilos in three minutes while eating chocolate! Ego ego ego …

In my current retreat business, I take clients to a 48 Hour Author retreat where they execute their first books. What those clients need is to understand their fear and self-doubt when it comes to taking the leap to write their first book; they need to learn how to structure, unpack and publish their intellectual property, and then to master a sales and marketing system that will bring them a never-ending stream of readers and clients.   But what they want is to get all this done in just 48 hours! Thus, the marketing of this retreat is framed as Ultimate 48 Hour Author but the reality once I get to serve my clients expands well beyond 48 hours.

In case you are thinking this is false advertising—it's not! We do help them execute their full content of the book during the 48 hours, but the preparation to the retreat requires them to really work on their mindset; the post-retreat period requires them to complete the publishing process and then invest as much time as possible to market and leverage their book to success.

You see, in most cases people will want a quick, easy, step-by-step solution to a problem that they wanted gone yesterday. This is the very first step of how you need to start thinking about your magnetic retreat offer.

Answer the following questions for yourself:
- What will my client walk away with when they are done with me?
- What problems do I solve for them?
- What does their ego want when I think about the frustration they are experiencing?

Now you are ready to craft your offer. Things to consider

include thinking about the support system you will put into place (not just the retreat) and how potentially you can have that client receive something after the retreat for having worked with you.

I'd like to introduce you to the table of value. <u>Visit here to check out what our retreat table looks like.</u>

A table of value is the best visual representation you can create for your retreat. This will be a document that will evolve over time as you find what works, what doesn't, what you should add, remove and how to continue tweaking it. It is really important to be able to talk about what each item in your table means and how you deliver it. It is not essential to describe everything to potential clients line by line, but it is important that you know it line by line as you will get those clients that will be more detailed and will ask you for this type of an explanation.

The secret to selling your retreat offer is to keep it all high level and outcome/result focused. I don't even share my table of value with clients until I have qualified them into my program and then it's just part of the logistics. During the sales process all my clients are interested in is that they get a book at the end of working with me and that I can be trusted, I have credibility and that they feel comfortable that I will take care of them along the way.

Nevertheless, having your table of value comes in handy to have it up on your website, to send to those that want the nitty-gritty and for you to itemise the massive value your retreat will add to the client's life.

Here are some key tips when building your own table of value:

- ensure you give your clients some tangible and intangible inclusions
- have one to three levels of entry—one offer only, two offers (one really cheap with an upgrade to

the premium one), three offers (low, mid and high entry into your retreat program); I'll explain these in a moment
- sexy (marketable) names for your inclusions and levels
- options for a payment plan and how your payment terms work
- a professionally drafted agreement by a lawyer that covers all the ins and outs when it comes to clients participating in your retreat program.

Let's look at these five in detail ...

Tangible and Intangible Inclusions

Since most retreat programs provide an intangible service and experience, it's a nice touch to add something that is tangible. First of all, what are intangibles?
- Time with you
- Email support
- Online communities
- Attendance at the retreat
- Workshop attendance

Here are some tangible ideas of what you can include:
- branded journals and stationery
- recommended books (preferably the one you have written)
- niche-related items (e.g. weight-loss niche—scales, heart rate monitor watch, pedometer, meal planner)
- retreat-related items (e.g. we had a *Survivor* theme like the reality TV show and we made head scarfs called Buffs for our attendees that they got to keep and take home with them as a memento)
- manuals with worksheets they will be using during the retreat

FULLY BOOKED RETREATS

- manuals or products they will use after the retreat (e.g. we give our authors at their retreat the Product Generator Manual that they can use once their book comes out and it teaches them exactly how to build their next products)
- branded T-shirts as a memento to take home after the experience
- post-retreat memento photo album you can make online from the photos taken during the retreat which you can send to your clients as a surprise and a reminder of the wonderful time they had.

Levels of Entry

One level of entry—in this case you simply have one line down your table of value which is your retreat program. You offer no other options—people are either in or out. This may be the way you will begin and certainly it was the way I began with our retreats, but I challenge you to think bigger. Why?

Two levels of entry—in this table of value you will have two columns with ticks along what clients will receive in Option 1 and then Option 2. I currently do this for my program. I have an online portal delivery of my intellectual property where clients get my system without any support bar the online communities. This is 90% cheaper than the retreat option which is what I aim to sell so that I can fully help people. Why I have the two options is that some people don't quite know if they are ready to take the full leap of faith into working with me. In this case I have the downsell option of getting them to commit to my online portal which gives them the option within twelve months to upgrade to the full retreat program and use the payment they made to the online portal as a deposit towards the retreat. This way I don't get a 'no' but a slightly open door plus a passive income sale for which I don't

11

need to do anything bar the onboarding component into the online portal. When clients see that doing it all alone is maybe not the best way to get the result they are after, they call us up to upgrade to the full handholding process.

Three levels of entry—here you end up with three columns with ticks along the inclusions of each level. The thinking behind this table of value and offer is that your aim is to get most people into the middle level. The brain loves three options: it works in chunks of three and 90% of the time you will find most will choose that middle level. Make sure you cater for that level the best, and make the lower one seem not enough and the high-end one super premium for those that want the most handholding and are most committed and serious about solving the problem in the fastest time possible.

Sexy Naming

When I speak of 'sexy' naming, all I mean is to make your inclusions and levels ego and wants focused. Goal setting does not sell; however, Future Design does. Time management does not sell, Multiply Your Time does. When you are writing titles and inclusions capitalise the first letter of the main words to make it pop more. I like using this in all my titles and subtitles so that it stands out more. Look up hypnotic words and phrases on Google and use them in all your naming of your inclusions, offers and the name of your retreat.

Payment Plans and Pricing

We live in a world where not many are financially savvy and cashflow is at crisis levels. For this reason being able to offer your retreat program with an upfront price and a payment plan price will help sell more. This brings me to answering one of the most commonly asked questions from my clients: Nat, how do I price my retreat? Do I just pull out a figure and run with it? NO!

First you need to do your research on your costs and negotiate prices with suppliers. Your cost for a retreat will definitely, at the very least, include accommodation and meals. But there is more. Think about how you can add extra value and really turn this into a no-brainer. In some cases we sweeten the deal with a flight if they pay the deposit and hand in the agreement on the day. We offer transfers to and from the airport, we have certain printed products and books we give each participant, and in authoring a book you can imagine we include all the other suppliers and 500 printed books delivered to their doorstep. Our retreat program has 50% hard costs that we need to pay out to other suppliers, but we also have negotiated these down as we bulk purchase from them all the time.

The second thing that I forgot to consider when I started running my own high-end retreat was the cost of marketing and travel. We run 30 half-day workshops nationwide to fill our four high-end retreats. These half-day workshops require us to invest in Facebook advertising, hire further venues, flights to travel, car hires, meals while away. They are what we call in the industry a loss leader. You lose at the front end but you end up making it up in the back end; therefore, you must build this into the pricing of your retreat as a cost. I didn't start advertising on Facebook immediately. I ran the program through its first six retreats purely through word of mouth and my warm network. Once that got exhausted I moved onto having more skin in the game. It was super scary but totally worth it as it allows you to build a well-oiled machine where you can stop worrying about getting bums on seats and focus on your delivery and conversion. The past four years we have consistently been converting at 10-15% from our half-day workshops which converts into seven figures plus in total revenue.

It is only when you have worked out these two costs that you are ready to price your retreat program. Take into consideration your time. Not just your time that it takes to execute the retreat and service clients, but the time it takes to promote, travel and deliver all the other activities that go into making the retreat possible. For us this would be the effort and time we put into delivering the half-day workshops and all the travel and logistics that we need to have in place to make them also just as awesome as our end product.

My recommendation is that you at least work on having 50-70% profit from your retreat price point. Definitely no less than 50%.

Once you have your price, decide on what the upfront payment would look like and then the payment plan time frame and rules. Upfront payment usually may have 5% of the total price of the retreat deducted and the payment plan would be the regular price split over a number of months. Please ensure that you collect a minimum payment to cover costs and a bit more before someone comes to your retreat. Preferably, you should be fully paid by the time you run your retreat, but sometimes this is not possible as it may be a high-end program that may need to be split over a longer period of time. In this case have you got anything to hold back on releasing until you have been paid? For us it is the books and the files to those books. Our agreements also are fair but firm and with diligent bookkeeping and great follow-up it is easy to ensure all goes according to plan.

WARNING: Do not allow clients to attend your retreat that have not paid you in full or the minimum required by the retreat. In my experience, having run retreats for five years at a high-end level, your heart will want to say yes to help the person but you should listen to your head which should always be a no. You will never see the money and each time I have thought I could trust the person, their word is good, every single time they have disappeared and not honoured their commitment or it has taken me four years to claim my funds, which brings me to ...

Your Agreement

Do not do this yourself. Do not copy it off someone else. Go to a lawyer and get one drafted up specific to your business and with the knowledge it is current and created for your particular circumstances and within your state's legislation. Note that sometimes legal agreements have no jurisdiction in other countries, but it's still good to have them completed as the act of signing an agreement is also commitment on both parties to uphold what has been agreed upon. Some things to consider in terms of conditions around your retreat:

- What happens if someone wants to cancel; do they get a refund of any sort?
- What happens if a client wants to move the date of their retreat? Do they get penalised as venue costs may already have been paid?
- Put in the terms of payment.
- Include protection of your intellectual property.
- Add in any disclaimers.

They are the main ones to make sure you cover and your lawyer will most likely have more suggestions and ideas you may not have thought of.

It is time now to create your first table of value. This and the date of your first retreat are the only things you will need to get out there and sell your retreat. To make your table of value graphically nice jump onto fiverr.com and hire someone to create something similar to what you saw on my table of value. That's all … do not create anything else until you have sold your first spot into your retreat!

Chapter 2
Sales Funnel Design
That Converts

The key to a fully booked retreat is a well-coordinated, planned and executed lead-up timeline where you have content going out, online and/or offline events that give people a taste of what it will be like when they choose to book their spot into your retreat. No one will part with their hard-earned cash unless they are able to understand what's in it for them!

A sales funnel does exactly that. It takes your ideal client on a journey of receiving value from you and getting to know you. Did you know that it takes 10-12 hours of content consumed by a potential buyer until they are ready to buy from you? How are you delivering this content? Here are some ideas:

- books- take anywhere from 2 – 5 hours to read
- videos (uploaded or live)- vary drastically
- blogging- 5 – 15 minutes
- webinars- usually 1 hour
- workshops- can be anywhere from 2 – 14 hours
- short online programs- 1 – 2 hours
- speaking gigs- 30 minutes – 2 hours.

A sales funnel does not need to be complicated. It can

contain as little as three steps and no more than five. So what does all of this mean? A three-step funnel may have free valuable content that you will offer in exchange for a person's email address as well as free content that you simply add value via a blog, videos, articles, webinars or speaking gigs. The following step can be an invitation to an online or offline event that is low cost (what we call the loss leader in your funnel) and the final step is your actual retreat. A five-step funnel could include extra steps whereby you may have a book that clients can buy for a low cost, an online event that leads into an offline event and finally your retreat. The simpler a sales funnel is, the easier it is to execute.

Personally, I do a ton of free content for my community and followers, have all my various books that people buy from me which I don't promote too heavily as the one thing that I focus my time most on is the half-day workshop (four hours) that is priced at $49 or $87 for a VIP ticket and that is what I look to fill successfully 30 times each year. This then converts into my high-end retreat clients which convert at 10-15% at that half-day workshop.

The key to creating your sales funnel is to start somewhere. Avoid getting excited and selling straight into your retreat if someone enquires about your retreat. The reason for this is that you haven't established enough value as yet and trying to take the easy road most of the time will lead to disappointment of the person thinking you are too expensive.

I like to say that any enquiry I get always leads to the half-day workshop. It's been famously said that all roads lead to Rome. Well, all my content, giveaways, speaking gig offers, social media posts and phone chats all lead to an invite to attend my half-day workshop. Check out one of my funnels here. It is a free e-book that I have as a bonus to my *Shut Up and Write Your First Book* book that asks for your email address, then invites you to the half-day workshop. This funnel was built inside ClickFunnels which is a monthly subscription platform that helps you build awesome-looking landing pages with a number of steps (the funnel steps).

By the end of my half-day workshop, I know wholeheartedly that if I haven't established value that I have given it my all; the potential client has also given themselves and me enough time to understand the retreat program and we end up knowing if there is a match or not to continue working together.

I am sure you have had situations in your business when people straight away want to ask the price of your service, program or retreat. I do as well. In these situations I try to get at least on a phone call to understand who this person is, what they are looking for, whether I can help and what would that look like if I do decide I can help them. They can push and push just for the price and in this case you have to give it to them—at which point you can just wave goodbye to ever working with them. I developed a little saying when it comes to this question: How much is your retreat?

If you are shopping on price, we are too expensive for you, if you are looking for value then let's have a conversation and see if we can help you.

Just think about this scenario: If I asked you to give me $1000 without any reason given, would you? Of course not. If I asked you to give me $1000 as a price for a Ferrari I need to get rid of, would you? You'd first think I was weird selling a Ferrari for $1000, but then you would do anything in your power to find that $1000 to buy the Ferrari off me as you know the return on investment when you onsell that will be hundreds of times more than $1000.

That is exactly how your clients will be looking to make a decision towards your retreat. They will need to see your retreat as the Ferrari that will ultimately bring back to them tens to hundreds of times return on investment into their lives.

This doesn't have to be measured just in monetary terms, as value and ROI can be measured in wellbeing, experience, happiness and fulfilment terms.

The Definition of 'Value'

Value is a feeling, not a calculation! Boom!

When I learnt about this distinction, it changed the way I looked at what I was offering. Especially as we are speaking about retreats in this book. Retreats are an experience and give us the power to trigger feelings within people, help them bond with others and walk away with a lifelong memory they will cherish and revisit in the future. That is something you cannot explain or calculate with $$$.

When you see your clients' faces at the end of their experience you will know. Make it your mission to keep improving the experience and bringing various 'wow' moments throughout. I will be sharing in a later chapter all about the fun stuff you can do at your retreat.

For now, it is time to get to work. Develop some content, talk about your passion, give away gold nuggets of information via video and in written format. Start building a buzz and a following around the problem that you solve for people. Remember, the more people you help achieve their dreams, yours will be taken care of as the natural result to all of this.

Chapter 3
Fully Booked Retreat

Bums on Seats!!! The most dreaded fear when it comes to running events. With the onset of the internet and with the ease of learning online, more and more people are choosing to stay at home and learn independently. Filling your retreat won't be a small feat, but I promise you it will be totally worth it. We are tribal creatures and if we can see the value in an experience and a faster way it can help us reach a solution, the answer will always be a 'Hell, yes!'. There are three ways you can get bums on seats at your retreat. We briefly touched on the sales funnel in the previous chapter, now I'd like to go into a little more detail of the three options you have to establish value with your ideal client. There are three roads to master and my suggestion is mastering one before moving onto another one. They are: running a half-day workshop; evergreen webinars; and sexy sessions. Let's break this down a little more:

Half-Day Workshop

My most successful strategy that I have worked now for over seven years is the tweaking and refinement of my half-day workshop. That is also why I have devoted a whole chapter to it, coming up. Briefly here, the half-day workshop is all about hosting a value-packed workshop where people get to meet you, get a feel for who you are, learn some awesome tips and tricks around the problem that you solve, and ultimately be given the opportunity to make a decision to work with you to fully solve the problem that you solve by saving themselves time, money and avoiding making mistakes trying to do it all alone.

There is a certain formula that works like magic when implemented that will see you convert 10-15% of your half-day participants into high-end paying clients. I will share that with you in the following chapter. If you would like to experience our half-day workshop click here. If you are not local to Australia simply contact us here and we can arrange to send you the professionally filmed footage of our full half-day workshop.

Evergreen Webinar

If you are not much of a face-to-face person and you don't like to travel around the country and world to meet your clients in workshops, the evergreen webinar funnel is a great option as a value builder that leads to a sales conversation on auto pilot. I learnt this system from Russell Ruffino from Clients on Demand and set up my evergreen webinar funnel that continues to bring in conversations with potential clients organically. I do not run Facebook ads to this funnel as I prefer to run my half-day workshops as my way of finding my ideal clients.

I have the evergreen webinar funnel advertised in all my social media profiles and any place people would look me up for more information. If you would like to take yourself through the experience of how it works and how it unfolds simply click here.

The idea of an evergreen webinar is that you will be able to establish value through a 45-minute online webinar presentation that is set up in a system that starts the webinar every hour, on the hour. The attendees think they have arrived 'just in time' for it and therefore the feeling is that they are live on the call with you after which they are given the opportunity to book a breakthrough session with you to discuss solving the problem they have. The system from start to finish looks like this:

Facebook Ad—Evergreen Webinar—Breakthrough Session—High-End Retreat

There are many intricate details when it comes to mastering this, like:

- how to run the Facebook ads
- setting up and growing your own Facebook group
- running a webinar
- creating your webinar slide deck
- setting up the booking pages, qualifying form and thank-you page
- how to run a breakthrough session that converts
- how to overcome objections and understand the sales process.

This is not something you would do on your own. Please speak to the experts at Clients on Demand who will help you with all of the above. I invested myself to learn it and love how easy Russell and his team make this.

Sexy Sessions

Part of the evergreen webinar model above would have this session; however, you can offer free or low-cost, high-value, outcome-focused sessions as a way to attract clients into your retreats. This is the slowest way and would require very high sales skills to convert clients into your retreat. Why?

- The potential client is just meeting you.
- It takes longer doing this one-on-one.
- You haven't established value at all yet via a workshop or a webinar.

Until you build infrastructure in your business whereby you have some of the aforementioned things set up, this method may be the initial way you will convert clients into your retreat. The one-on-one conversation plays part in all three methods; you cannot escape it, so you must master it for success.

The first thing you must ensure is to sell the potential client into this session. They will not give you their time just because you say it's free. There are two things you need to clear up for the person when they are considering chatting to you.

1. The name of your session
2. The main takeaways for the client when they spend the time with you

Remember, no one books in for a sales call. There needs to be value they will receive for spending time with you. The sale is just a natural next step if there is a fit and a need to further help the person with your system.

Here is an example of a name and takeaways from a low-cost session I used to offer a few years ago:
Name: Product Generator Power Session

What you walk away with:
- ideas of how to package and produce your expertise into a product that thousands can buy
- how to add value to your clients in the form of products

- how products increase and truly leverage your credibility
- a plan on how to launch and create your first product
- make more money by bundling your services with products
- reduce selling your time for money
- generate passive income so you can operate your business internationally.

I would then offer this to a limited number of people, thus introducing the Law of Scarcity, and I offered it at a low entry point (not for free!) so that people had skin in the game and actually turned up for the session. At the end of the session if we both felt that there would be value in implementing and completing the above takeaways in a systematic way, I would take the time to explain to that prospect how we could work together to make it happen. In the retreat sense, I may have offered for them to join me at my next Product Generator Retreat to build the product of their choice while being supported and guided every step of the way.

The trick with sexy sessions is that you keep evolving and adjusting what you can see works and what obviously doesn't. Take the time to learn a sales system that will support you with the structure of this session and how to overcome objections even before they arise.

The time and energy that you spend refining one of these three methods will pay back in truckloads of sales and retreat participants—you will never need to stress about bums on seats and you can focus on improving your delivery and experience at your retreats.

Chapter 4
Half-Day Workshop Format

The fastest way to grow your business, especially the number of participants at your retreat, is to get out there and meet them, add value to them and show them how you can solve their problem easily and systematically. Retreats are a face-to-face delivery and that is why I believe meeting your potential clients face to face makes the progress into the next step a lot easier than if they meet you first online or on a phone call. That's why when I mentioned evergreen webinars in the previous chapter, I also believe they nicely progress into a sale of an online program. Start online, finish online, start offline, finish offline is the thinking behind this.

I could write a whole book by itself just on how to run a half-day workshop masterfully (I may do this next ... keep an eye out for one), but in this chapter I want to share some hot tips with you when it comes to your half-day workshop. Here are 10 things you must plan for and consider:

- When to run your half day, what time and what days of the week.
- How often, how many and where to host your half day.
- How to look for venues and what to know about them.
- What equipment you will need.
- How to design your PowerPoint so it wows and sells.

- How to set up your room for the workshop.
- Crew.
- How to set up your pre- and post-logistics of the event.
- How to follow up.
- Running ads to fill the room.

That pretty much looks like the chapters of a book I could write! Funny about that. Let me give you some key hacks that will help you get some answers around the abovementioned points.

When to Run Your Half-Day Workshop

After years of testing and tweaking, I believe I have discovered what works for my business and life. This may be different for yourself. I will share my reasons why I do my events when I do.

I like to run my half-day workshops on a Tuesday, Wednesday or Thursday outside of school and national holidays and any major events in a city we are going to. My reasons are:

1. I don't like working on weekends. I used to do it a lot and then every week blended into the next and I felt I never got a break. Now if your niche market all have jobs, weekend might be the best time. My niche market are entrepreneurs and they normally are very flexible. I do have those that request weekend, but I don't want to do it, so I don't. My retreats, however, are on a weekend, four times a year, and those weekends are devoted and locked in years in advance.

2. I run the workshop 9 a.m. – 1 p.m. The reason is that I don't cater for lunch and people can go to lunch straight after. When you are running a low-cost event, your costs must be kept low as you will still be losing money at the front end. We sometimes provide

coffee and other times not, depending on the cost of the venue.

3. I don't like doing them on Mondays or Fridays as people's mindsets are in start-up or finish-up mode. Also Mondays allow us to travel up to an interstate city and get ready for three days of events (as I like to cluster them and get my work done in blocks). Fridays I also like to have free (partly because 90% of Fridays I have a day off and have three-day weekend) but the other reason is because it's another working day where you can finalise your sales before people have gone into weekend mode and are not taking action.

How Often, How Many and Where

I've mentioned it a few times already and I will mention it again. I run 30 half-day workshops to fill four retreats per year. They are normally divided into two national tours in autumn and spring when most people do go to events. Running and filling events in winter and summer is harder. Summer more than winter is a no-go zone. You may think 30 is a lot of events, but when you think about the sales funnel it's not.

Let's look at some conservative numbers: 30 events, let's say with 30 attendees at each event. If you are getting a 10% conversion rate, that means you will get three retreat attendees at each event, bringing you to 90 per year. Multiply that by the price of your retreat program and you will be well on the way into high six if not seven-figure revenue.

So where do you run them? When I started out it was multiples in my home city, well spaced out so that I could fill the room with success. There will come a time when you will need to spread your wings and go to places where you have no warm market and tap into the power of advertising and collaborations.

Go to big cities that have more affluent demographics. Usually capital cities should always be on your list and then some bigger ones or higher affluence. For example, Brisbane is a capital city in Queensland; however, only an hour up or down the coast are the Sunshine Coast and Gold Coast. People that live in these smaller areas with lots of people are more affluent; however, they will not travel into Brisbane for an event. So we go to them and I would have to say, they are one of our highest converting locations in Australia. We have trialled other big population towns with not as much affluence and while they love what we do and get a ton of value, our conversion rate and results has not been great, thus deciding not to return there in the future.

You will need to work out depending on the price of your retreat, the ideal client profile and where they live, and then create a calendar of events for the full year that you will execute to fill your dream retreat program.

Venue Secrets Unlocked

As your half-day workshop is a place you will lose money to promote and hold, you must be mindful of those front-end expenses. How you choose venues will depend where you are at in this journey. When I was starting out and didn't have as much cashflow or confidence in what I was selling, I used to hire places that I could use for free or very low cost. Of course this builds a certain perception. That didn't matter as I knew I was passionate about what I was offering and that would come through when I made the offer.

Initially I went to function rooms in pubs or restaurants which can give you the room for free as they assume people will buy food or drinks when there. If you tell the venue that you want to book a few dates ahead of time, they may be more accommodating too. Sometimes they may choose to even sponsor your event.

As you become more established and increase your cash flow, booking venues at hotels where you can also stay the night before as you travel in is ideal. Hotels are the perfect places set up for functions and events. Watch out though for all the extra things they want to sell you, such as expensive tea and coffee per person, morning tea, projector hire and even sometimes whiteboard hire. I personally hate paying for these extras and we also do our best to negotiate a price that fits our budget. We also let them know we intend to return, all going well with our experience with them. I suggest invest in your own projector—it will save you thousands in hire. I bought mine for home use years ago and 10 years on I still use it in venues that won't include it.

Equipment Essentials

Venues usually have all the equipment you should need to run an event but I simply don't trust that they will have everything. Here are the extra things that I always have with me:

- my own whiteboard markers that I love (theirs are often overused and don't work properly)
- my own projector if I need to (you will know this ahead of time)
- my own clicker to change the PowerPoint slides
- my own powerful Bluetooth speaker (they may have audio which is great but sometimes it may not work properly, in which case I connect my computer audio to my speaker). I also use the speaker for some background music at the beginning, end and during the break. It would be good to have two speakers so you don't have to swap the Bluetooth between

devices. The second one doesn't have to be as big or powerful as it's just for some background music

- my own powerboard with USB ports on it. We have a lot of technology devices that need to be on charge during the event. Take your own board and you will never need to worry
- my spare iPhone and iPad. I play music from my spare iPhone through the second speaker and the iPad is used to register people at the door while my computer is ready with the presentation and hooked up with the powerful Bluetooth speaker. I also use my iPad to put on a speaking timer so that I pace myself through the presentation and I never run over time
- all my paperwork like name tags, list of attendees, release form, sign-up sheet, any handouts
- pencil case with highlighter, marker, pens, a few notepads if the venue doesn't have them.

PowerPoint Design

My current half-day presentation is 90 slides long. You may think that is too long, but it contains many visuals and models that are shared throughout. I have refined and adjusted it more than 10 times since I started running my half-day event. I have run my half day now close to 150 times. Here are the key areas that you need to speak about in your presentation, in order:

- Your Title Slide (name of workshop with your logo and a nice image).
- Logistics Slide (event logistics and timing with what you will cover).
- Why Slide (why you are here slide. Get the room to talk to each other and then unpack this on the board).
- Your Story Slide deck (tell your zero-to-hero story

with a purpose to teach and talk about mistakes you have made and how you have overcome them). Reveal the price point of your retreat but don't talk about it in detail.

- Three Key Points you will cover today.
- Cover the Three Key Points (in one of them try to workshop something with the group—show them how easy it is).
- Cover one point before the break and have the Call to Action for a Qualifying conversation straight after the powerful group workshopping.
- Share Success Stories with examples and testimonial videos.
- Show your retreat experience with a professional two- to three-minute video once you can create this.
- Present your Offer and payment plans.
- Repeat the Call to Action.
- Have a slide with a Bonus only for the first person to sign up (e.g. for us we give the first person to sign up a return flight to their retreat).
- Finish with an inspiring action Quote.

Room Set Up for Your Workshop

Every time I walk into a venue, I end up resetting the room to ensure my success on the day. That is also why I like to get into a venue room no later than 7:30 a.m. for the 9 a.m. start as I know participants have been told to start arriving from 8:30 a.m. for registration and some of them most likely will come even earlier and some super late. Nevertheless, the time between 7:30 – 8 a.m. is used to rejig things how I like.

When we stay at a hotel the night before, we always ask if we can set up the night before as the next morning we can just focus on hooking up the computer and getting the final tiny bits organised. If you can do this, I recommend it every single time.

When I walk into a venue, the first thing I look at are the chairs and the way things are placed in the area where I will stand and then the registration and products display area. Most of the time, no matter how many instructions you have given the venue, these things need tweaking so they suit what you like.

Adjust the chairs first. The set-up of the chairs will depend on how many people are coming to the event. If you have 20 or less participants set the room up in a U-shape. It looks fuller and everyone can see each other. It's a lot more inclusive and no one is turning their backs to others. Over 20 participants, I always go to theatre style where the chairs are offset so that I can see everyone's face. I also like spreading people out as I know I don't like to be squeezed into a row full of people.

I then ensure all my technology and the front of the room where I will be using the space most is set to my comfort and also so that the full audience can see the whiteboard and PowerPoint easily and I don't trip on any cords.

While I do this my crew or my husband will set up my products table at the back of the room. They also set up the registration table which becomes the crew table during the workshop. Once all of this is done I look at everything as a whole and make any tweaks as required.

Crew

Having crew really helps with the whole process and experience of the workshop. In the early days, I didn't have anyone and did it all myself. I still managed, but the key benefits of having crew are:

1. You look more professional and established.

2. They take care of things you should not be thinking about.
3. They are your testimonials in the room and often convert people that may be on the fence.
4. They are there for questions when you are caught up with other people.
5. They help you set up and pack up.
6. They can offer feedback at the end once it's all done and give you some hints on the people they have chatted to. Also, they may be able to reveal some questions they get asked that you may not be aware of.
7. They can mingle and build rapport with more people, especially at the beginning of the day when everyone is cold.

Pre- and Post-Logistics for Your Workshop

Three years ago I hired a virtual assistant from the Philippines to help me with the admin side of my business as my husband didn't like doing it and we were best utilised as the experts and mentors in the business. If you would like to get a virtual assistant simply post a job up on www.upwork.com and interview those that apply to see who is a good fit. I am still with the one and only I have ever had.

We use a free project management program www.asana.com to ensure all of our pre- and post-logistics for our workshops get executed consistently and at the right time. We also use Asana for other task management and we run various templates for new clients, retreats, book launches and masterclasses.

If you are going to put in the big effort that it takes to execute 30 half-day workshops every year, you must make your system streamlined so that you are not missing opportunities or people are not knowing what will happen next. There are

12 tasks logistically we need to complete to close off each half-day workshop. Here is what a sample template of this looks like:

- Client buys a ticket—they get an automated receipt and information on the event from the ticketing system. Virtual assistant picks up these sales and builds attendee lists in a spreadsheet for each city.
- The event is set up in Asana with city and data and the tasks are populated from our template with who needs to complete each task and when so they get timely reminders.
- 10 days out—a customised logistics email goes out to participants where we ask them to send us their postal address and as a thank you we give them one of my books in ebook version. My assistant again populates addresses in the spreadsheet and emails out the free ebook as a thank you.
- Three days out—we email the logistics email once again in case they missed it and also SMS all participants with logistics to get a confirm reply Yes or No if they are attending (we use www.textmagic.com for SMS management as I don't have to be involved in it).
- 24 hours out—we email the logistics once more as people don't clear their emails regularly so they have it in their newer emails. We also SMS once more only those that have not responded Yes or No to the first SMS at three days out.
- Event day—participants register at the door. We grab any missing addresses and get a release form for photos signed off. We have printed sticky name tags and those that are VIP tickets receive a personally signed book from me. I personally love being at the registration desk as I can meet people as they walk in

and sign their book. I believe it builds rapport quickly and it's a nice touch.

- After the event a thank-you email with any resources promised goes out before 6 p.m. that afternoon.
- My assistant sends a No Show email to the no shows with filmed footage of the event which we have professionally filmed in the past.
- My assistant adds all participants in our database correctly.
- My assistant adds all participants in our Send Out Cards system through which we upload a photo in a postcard and post it to all attendees so they get it a week after the event as a memento from our time together.
- My husband initiates a five sequence email series post event that covers common objections and other doubts they may be having to taking action towards writing their book.
- We text all the qualifying chat participants on the second day after the event as our Fast Mover price expires 48 hours after the workshop. By this stage if people are in, they are in; if you haven't heard you probably never will.

Those are the main steps with a half-day workshop. You may have more or less—it all depends. We sometimes have removed some steps and other times added more. Keep looking at ways of getting your turn up rates improved and your conversion higher.

Following Up

I've touched on follow-up briefly in the point before. Here I'd like to make some other distinctions and things you must be fast at. When you have a qualifying chat with someone after the event and you have promised to send them information, such as an agreement, bank details, etc., do it fast. This is the first task to complete even before your thank-you email goes out. I even text the person that I have emailed them what I have promised. I also friend the hot prospects on Facebook the same day, so I stay top of mind with them.

On the day that the 48 hours bonus expires send a courtesy message that this is the case and always tell people you are on call for those 48 hours so they can contact you at any time to ask questions. Don't expect everyone will be courteous back. Most people that are a 'No' will not tell you. They will just ignore the message. Just know after 48 hours who is in, is in and who is not, never will be. It is very rare that I have had people return or even forget that the Fast Mover price was expiring.

Running Ads to Fill the Room

There will come a time when you will exhaust your warm network and need to start building an audience that has never heard of you. This is where paid advertising comes in. Whatever you do, do not do this yourself. Paid advertising is a specialty, just like whatever you specialise in. It has many intricacies that us lay people don't understand. Hire an expert on a monthly retainer that will help you get this right. Get referrals and recommendations when choosing who to work with. Talk to their clients and preferably hire someone that is located in your country.

A few things to bear in mind with paid advertising:
1. You must practise patience in the early days—it takes time to test and measure, gain traction and work the algorithms that are in Facebook.
2. You will need to bring out fresh content and work

alongside your expert to ensure that you get results sooner rather than later.

3. Decide on a budget per event and see how many bums on seats that gets you. Once you are more confident, you may want to up that further to scale up.

4. Only do paid advertising once you have exhausted your warm network and make at least 10K in your niche.

5. This is a long-term strategy that you should be doing alongside your organic strategies to get bums on seats.

Once paid advertising works well for you, put your efforts into refining what you do and if it ever slows down or stops working, make sure you pull out all the other ways you can get bums on seats outside of paid ads. Read *Bums on Seats* if you want to get some ideas.

I told you I could write a book with the amount of information and experience I have when running half-day workshops. Once you get this part right, the rest is easy and super fun. Now go and schedule your calendar of half-day workshops.

Chapter 5
Team Work is Dream Work

Hosting retreats requires a lot of planning, problem solving and management to ensure success and a wonderful time for your participants. That is why in most cases you should not be doing them alone. Just as I recommended having crew for your half-day workshop, having crew at your retreat is just as important. Perfect retreat crew are past participants who have already been part of your retreat program. If you are just starting out, ask fellow business friends or people that you are close with if they would lend a hand.

One thing to consider is the cost of having a crew member at your retreat and whether you will get them to take care of the accommodation and meal expenses. You may choose to partly cover these costs for them. Here is a look inside my crew instructions I share with those that may want to crew.

Ultimate 48 Hour Author Crew Instructions

Thank you so much for agreeing to crew at the next Ultimate 48 Hour Author retreat. Your help is much appreciated and we know that you will gain a lot out of this experience, having it from a different perspective this time around. This document explains our expectations during retreat from you so that you feel guided and are aware of the exact role that you are playing.

As a crew member the most important thing is to observe the authors' emotional wellbeing. There will be nervous, quiet, loud and reserved personalities. We want to make sure everyone gets equal attention and has all their questions answered. You, being a previous Ultimate 48 Hour Author, would know that the beginning of this journey is filled with uncertainty and fear. Make sure you share that with the authors so they know they are not alone in feeling uneasy if they are, especially at the beginning of the weekend.

The investment in this experience is $500AUD which covers a fraction of the accommodation and meal expenses (we cover the additional $300 plus drinks expenses of having you there). The $500 is payable anytime pre-retreat and up to 30 days post-retreat (insert your payment details here). You investment is tax deductable and includes GST.

The benefits to you are:
- networking opportunity with high-level individuals
- possible discovery of collaborative partners
- past crew have gained clients from being there and helping
- listening to the retreat content and teachings from a different angle and perspective second time around— always more insights to be had
- impromptu mentoring and questions answered about your business from us (one-on-one time)
- ability to observe operations from the point of running your own retreats/events in the future
- some time away from the real world and social fun with like-minded people.

Below is a run sheet of the weekend where I will note in italics the things you should do at various times. Sometimes we allocate different roles between crew members but this will be discussed at retreat depending on people's skills and strengths. The tasks below are generalised as things you should look out to do.

Ultimate 48 Hour Author Retreat Run Sheet

Friday

Transfers to venue begin around 9 – 9:30 a.m. at Melbourne airport when we pick up interstate participants. Sometimes our crew help us with an extra car to do the pick-up with our two cars. You will be asked if this is possible ahead of time. If you are doing this then we meet at the Waiting Area just off the long-term car park exit off the freeway at 9 a.m. and await to hear that all authors are ready to collect in front of Park Royal. If you are not doing a drive through the airport, please arrive at the venue 11:30 – 12. Address of venue will be shared ahead of time.

You will have your own room at the venue. Please help out with setting up of the training room at this stage. Nat or Stu will guide you as to what is to be done so set-up is quick and efficient. Usually setting up pull-up banners, book tables, author product and books, and retreat booklet on the desks. Here are some photos of how our training room is set up ...

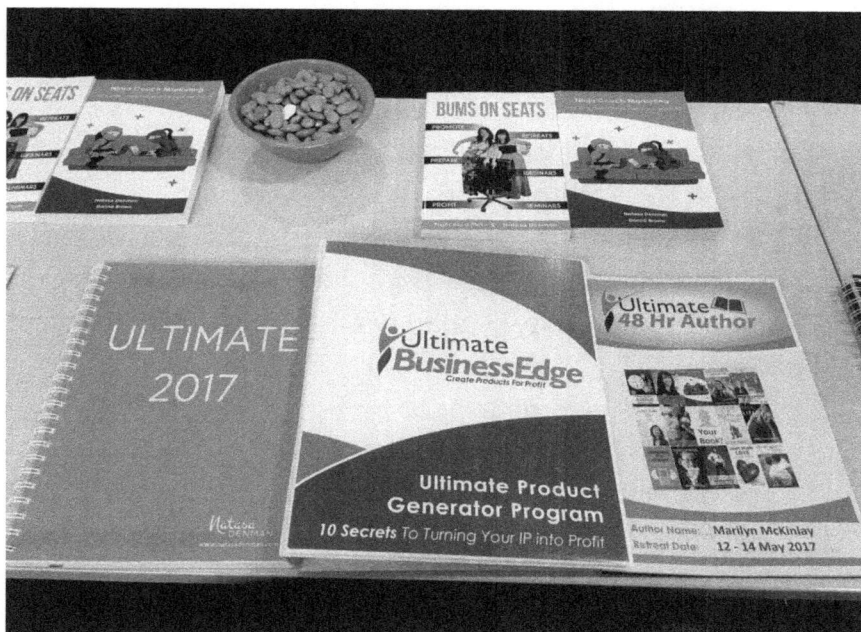

2:00 – 2:30 p.m.—Welcome and Move In (It's recommended you are at the venue by 12)

You may be able to move into your room earlier—we will advise official start time as sometimes it's earlier. Your role is to chase up any latecomers via the participant list. Give Nat ETA of people not there yet and advise all as we are about to begin the retreat. There will be registration just before the official start time—please give each author a Sticky Name Tag and get them to sign the Release Form. Point out where they are sitting according to where their retreat booklet with their name is placed.

* You will be given a list with all authors' contact details and a map of where everyone is located around the venue (their room).

2:30 – 4:00—Meet and Greet (mock-up covers critique)

By all means participate in the feedback and brainstorming here and you will be asked to introduce yourself after the authors have done their intros. Your book will be flashed up on the PowerPoint—please tell us about it and then add on what is the best way the authors can utilise you over the weekend (your strengths) and your best piece of advice you can give them to succeed. So maybe a mistake you made they can avoid always works best or something to alleviate their fear they are feeling right now.

4:00 – 4:15—Afternoon Tea

As we play the song to go to the first recording hour, make sure you usher the authors and urge them to go to their rooms and start recording. They tend to want to chat and waste a lot of the first recording hour.

4:30 – 5:30—Recording Hour 1

5:30 – 6:15—Teach Segment 1

If you are on social media duties please live stream during teach segments either on my personal profile, Ultimate Business Support Group, Author Your Way to Riches group or the Ultimate 48 Hour Author fan page. Do the live streams for at least 5 – 10 minutes and choose a sexy grabbing title before you go live. Nat's iPhone code is (enter your code here).

6:15 – 6:30—Break

Let authors know when break is over and to go to their rooms for another recording hour.

6:30 - 7:30—Recording Hour 2 *(During this hour the crew will have a pre-dinner drink, debrief and chat at a selected location of the venue.)*

Any authors that have not come out to dinner by 7:40, go to their room and let them know we have started dinner.

7:30 – 8:30—Dinner

After dinner we will have the Pre-Launch Sales segment which we have refined to be a lot faster as all authors are requested to set up their techie bits from home. There will be some that are not set up and will need our help.

This is a 12-minute video I sent them to set themselves up— might be helpful to watch so you understand what we have asked them to do and if you can help them out:

8:30 – 10:30—Optional Extra work and Mentoring to Catch up

10:30 – Midnight—Spa O'clock (Suggested Bed O'clock—Pumpkin Hour)

Fun times in the spa—if you are not up to it and would like to go to bed by all means please excuse yourself and go and rest.

Saturday

7:45 – 8:30—Breakfast

Please be at breakfast at the latest by 8 a.m. as if anyone is running late we would like to knock on their door 8:15 a.m. as we start 8:30 a.m. sharp.

8:25 a.m.—give all those still at breakfast table a five-minute warning

8:27 a.m.—play the song in the training room loud

8:30 – 9:15—Teach Segment 2

9:15 – 10:15—Recording Hour 3

Put theme song on from 10:10 a.m. in the training room if we are not allowed to walk around venue with music. If we are then do the walk around.

10:15 – 10:30—Morning Tea

10:30 – 11:15—Teach Segment 3

11:15 – 12:15—Recording Hour 4

12:15 – 1:15—Lunch

1:15 – 2:15—Recording Hour 5

After the long break which some may have worked almost three hours we want to make sure we get everyone back from 2:10 for the 2:15 start.

2:15 – 3:00—Teach Segment 4

3:00 – 3:15—Afternoon Tea

3:15 – 4:15—Recording Hour 6 *You may be asked to do the*

Sunday roster with Nat for chats with Blaise, photos with Kev and transfers back to airport.

4:15 – 5:00—Teach Segment 5

5:00 – 6:30—Relax

6:30 – 7:00—Pre-Dinner Mingle (Fancy Dress Parade and Photos)

We normally gather from 6 p.m. in the pre-dinner area, sometimes for some cocktail drinks, and take lots of photos in our fancy dress attire. This is lots of fun so we'd love to see you in your outfit for the night.

7:00 – 8:00—Dinner

No work after dinner just socialising.

8:00 – 10:00—Optional Extra work and Mentoring to Catch up

10:00 – Midnight—Spa O'clock (Suggested Bed O'clock—Pumpkin Hour)

Sunday

7:15 – 8:00—Breakfast

Please be at breakfast at the latest by 7:30 a.m. as if anyone is running late we would like to knock on their door 7:45 a.m. as we start 8:00 a.m. sharp.

7:55 a.m.—give all those still at breakfast table a five-minute warning

7:57 a.m.—play the song in the training room loud

8:00 – 8:45—Teach Segment 6

8:45 – 9:45—Recording Hour 7 (Check out of room 9:45-10:00 a.m.)

Pack your stuff from your room and place luggage in training room and check yourself out.

10:00 – 10:45—Teach Segment 7 and Finale Exercises

10:45 – 11:00—Blaise speak to group collectively

11:00—Kev takes Group Yay photo

11:30—Finish approx 3:00 Photoshoot and Publisher Conversations (15 minutes each with Kev and Blaise) Please note: Local authors go first and depart or may not have photos depending on retreat numbers. Local authors may need to go into the Montmorency Studio for their photos.

After the Group Yay photo it gets kind of messy. People everywhere either chatting to Blaise, photos with Kev, testimonials with one of you or Stu and other while they wait doing some more work. We will have a pre-departure checklist everyone needs to be ticked off on before they leave. It looks like this:

Name	Feedback Blaise	Photos	Photo with Nat	Group Shot	Testimonial	Ezypay
Pre-Departure Checklist (Sunday)						
Svetlana Williams						
Marilyn McKinlay						
Gill Walker						
Natasha Eli						
Deanne Banks						
Gregie Dennis						
Kitty Cheng		Melb				
Zoe Quin		Melb				
Kristina Herreen		Melb				

If you are asked to take Testimonials please follow these instructions:
1. Do it either on Nat or Stu's iPhone.
2. Hold phone Landscape.
3. Position the author either in front of U48A Banner or nice scenery light in their face (do not have light behind them like a window or brightness).
4. Ask for a 30-second to one-minute testimonial …
5. Script 'Hi, my name is (Author Name) soon to be author of (their book) and I just completed the Ultimate 48 Hour

Author retreat ....' Insert what they loved about it (best things to say are was it value for money, something about the system, favourite part, how fast it was, easy, etc.) Thank you at the end.

You can start and stop a few times if you feel the author is nervous; make them feel at ease and start again. Please delete out the flops and keep the good one only.

We can start packing up after the Yay Group photo has been taken. If you can stack the books from the display table and just put everything in one pile, pull down the banner, fold the tablecloth, Nat and Stu will finish the rest of the packing as it's easier to find things when we get home and unpack. Estimate that you may be leaving the venue around 3 p.m. If you need to leave earlier just let us know and we can work around that.

Thank you so much for taking part in this Ultimate 48 Hour Author retreat. We know you will walk away with some amazing new close relationships, friendships, possibly collaborations and perhaps even clients. If you enjoyed yourself and saw value in this experience we invite you to come back again in the future.

Lots of Love

Nat and Stu xxx

Your crew instructions will most likely be different but I highly recommend you have them typed up in a system such as the one you have just read. It may start off being just one page, but trust me, it will grow as you work out the things you need and how to best communicate that with your crew. Share these instructions well ahead of time and have them printed for your crew when they arrive. People love having direction and details which removes the need for them asking you a ton of questions while you should be focusing on your delivery.

Retreat participants find the crew super helpful and enjoy having someone else for support. We have always had wonderful feedback regarding the different crew and experts we have brought in to help out during the retreat.

Now it's your turn. Make a list of who you can ask to crew for you, both at your next half-day workshop or retreat. Then get to creating your crew instructions.

Chapter 6
Breathtaking Venues

As I write this my husband is on his way to check out another venue for our next retreat. Venues both for workshops and retreats are a never-ending search and refinement themselves. It is really important to have back-up venues and options when it comes to running events. Having your heart set just on a particular one is a recipe for disaster.

Normally the retreats that you will be running won't be corporate-size groups which means you may need to book your venue a month or two ahead of time. The reason for this is venues may have a minimum size group they may want to take and you may not know your total number until much closer to your retreat. Later bookings mean that you may or may not get into the venue you like. We have six to seven retreat venues that we can call upon and are still searching for more.

The first thing to create when searching for a venue is your non-negotiables list. This way you are clear on what questions you need to ask and what to look for when you arrive to check out the venue. Sometimes visiting a venue is not possible, so I would ask them to send me lots of photos of what I need to see. Here is an example of our list of non-negotiables:

Venue Requirements for Ultimate 48 Hour Author Retreat

- Individual rooms for all attendees for two nights (Fri and Sat)
- Private conference room that fits the number of attendees in U-shape set up with audio visual
- Smaller breakout room or private space available for mentoring
- Access from 11 a.m. Friday for crew and event set-up, attendees from midday > 1 p.m.
- Access until 4 p.m. Sunday if photography, 2 p.m. without > check out of rooms by 10 a.m. okay
- Dedicated events team/manager
- Up to $(Your Budget) per person is our budget
- Full catering service for all meals
- Friday afternoon tea and dinner
- Saturday breakfast, morning tea, lunch, afternoon tea and dinner
- Sunday breakfast, morning tea and lunch

We also have a look at the venue in terms of its surroundings and whether they have a spa, sauna, gym and a pool. These are not super crucial but it does help with what we communicate to our participants.

Share with excitement the venue photos, once you have it locked in, with your participants that are already coming and generally on social media. Beautiful photos attract new interest in what you are doing and you may get new enquiries from interested parties.

Another idea if you don't yet have a retreat experience video that I had mentioned to run in your half-day workshop is to set up a movie trailer using iMovie on your phone. If you don't have an iPhone ask a friend if you can borrow theirs for a few minutes. What you need is to have the images of the venue and some other images, maybe of you speaking, and plug those into an iMovie template on the phone and create some words in the sections where there are slides with words. iMovie then compiles it all and creates an emotionally driven trailer that you can download and put on your presentation. This way you can share this on your website, social media and in your workshop. Completely free! Once you have a budget for a professional video, get a videographer to come to your retreat and take some footage to compile a video.

Staying Calm

When you work with people at different venues, please practise patience and ask for help as you need it. Running events can be stressful, but a stress-head cannot solve problems as they may arise. Be nice to venue staff and they will do whatever you like. Remember, build rapport as you may be going back there a few times. If you burn your bridges you will create that much more stress in your life. Always look to turn something into a positive rather than a negative. It should feel like you have arrived home when you walk into a venue that you have used before. The best result from being nice and staying calm is that venues will give you bonuses and extra-special treatment as they enjoy working with you.

Location Tips

We attract 90% of our clients from interstate as, after all, we run events all over the country. Therefore, having a venue no longer than 60 minutes from the airport is important for transfers. We do go the extra mile to pick up and drop off our interstate clients at the airport. Ensure you have a strong system around arrivals and departures and how you communicate this to those coming in on a flight.

You may choose to do your retreat in another state that is not your home. If this is the case then you still need to think about transfers from the airport there and your own luggage that you will need to carry for your retreat. We prefer to have our clients come to us as my mum takes care of our three kids while we host our weekend retreats. Also we have so much product and books that we need to take with us that lugging it on a flight would not be very easy. We do live in a capital city with an airport 30 minutes from home so that makes it handy to have it hosted locally for us.

Understanding your venue costs will help you in planning and pricing your retreat. Ensure you find an average cost to plan with. Sometimes you may come under and other times go over that average, which is to be expected. Now get out there and check out some venues for your retreat program.

Chapter 7
Engaging Format

Retreats are an experience like no other. The difference between an average retreat and a Wow retreat experience is the element of surprise. You do not need to reveal all that will happen at the retreat. Your participants just need to know the outcome they will come away with once having finished the retreat. Aside from your expertise and format that you plan to deliver, here are some other 'wow' factors to consider in your planning:

- retreat song and theme
- ice breaker games with a hidden meaning as a lesson
- group activities
- games related to your theme
- social time/fancy dress
- workbook with handouts
- your run sheet.

Let's break these down in more detail ...

Retreat Song and Theme

This was the very first thing I introduced to my retreat since day one. Actually, it was the song first and the theme came from retreat #7. Songs are wonderful anchors that take people back to a time when they did something or were with someone. Having a song that will remind your participants of their retreat experience is super powerful. The song also aids as a timing strategy. You play it when you want everyone to come back to the training room, at the start of each day or to sit down after a break.

When choosing songs, look at the lyrics, the style of the song and how it sounds when played loudly. It's better to choose songs people would know and love already. Choosing one that they have never heard may take a little time for them to get used to.

Next comes the theme. I like to tie in the song with the relevant theme which we then use to dress up in fancy dress on night two of the retreat. You can also play out the full theme all throughout the retreat like we did recently with our *Survivor* theme. I'll explain more on that in the Games section.

Here are some ideas of songs and themes we have used to get you started in thinking for yourself:
- 'Fame' by Irene Cara with the theme: FAME
- 'Final Countdown' by Europe with the theme: SPACE
- 'Heaven' by Belinda Carlisle with the theme: ANGELS
- 'We are the Champions' by Queen with the theme: OLYMPICS
- 'Rock Around the Clock' with the theme: ROCK'N'ROLL
- 'You've Got the Power' by SNAP with the theme: HAWAII IN DUBAI
- 'Freedom' by George Michael with the theme: FREEDOM
- 'Fly Away' by Lenny Kravitz with the theme: FLYING
- 'Survivor' by Destiny's Child with the theme: SURVIVOR

Ice Breakers

As you begin your retreat, all participants may feel a little anxious, nervous, excited and uneasy, all at the same time.

That is why having a song, a theme and then the icebreaker to kick off unites everyone and makes them laugh and let go of their inhibitions. You can call all these the warm-up.

I love discovering fun ice breaker games that have a hidden meaning behind them. We do them because they are fun, but at the same time they are making a big point that we can discuss after the fact. The ones I use involve putting a straw through an uncooked potato (look it up on YouTube and then let people do it). You will find they try all sorts of things and most won't succeed. At this point, after giving them three minutes to try, coach them how to do it successfully and then make a powerful point with that exercise. There are always a few laughs when I pull out the potatoes, interesting ways people succeed and then a big 'aha' once they know how to do it properly.

Exercises with candles are fun (just be careful with fire) and other stuff I am sure you can google or ask others if there are any tricks or fun stuff they can do during training. People love to play and learn. You don't need to do 10 – 15 of these, just choose 2 – 3 powerful ones they can remember.

Group Activities

The power of the group and mastermind has been said is second to none. People learn from each other, love to support one another and come up with a variety of ideas when in a group setting. That is also why retreats are so powerful and transformational. Think about your system and model and work out if there is any way you can get people into a group activity.

For us it is the pre-launch segment of our authors' books on the Friday night of their retreat. After dinner we take our desserts to the training room and we collectively help each other to pre-launch the books being written. This exercise and fun carries through the full retreat and we get a total amount of books pre-sold by the Sunday night. We celebrate people's first book sale and keep checking in on the progress as the retreat continues. For our participants this gives them a sense that they have support from their network, people are interested in their book and also they can start seeing funds coming into their PayPal account for those pre-sales.

What is a group activity you can bring into your program?

Games Related to Your Theme

As I mentioned earlier people learn best through play and experiential situations. If you want to take it up another notch, tie in your theme with some related quick and fun games. Here are a couple of examples:

When we had the Olympics theme, we created an opening and closing ceremony, a tally of those that pre-sold the most books, so we awarded Bronze, Silver and a Gold medal at the end of the retreat, we had a best-dressed Olympian, we dressed up our training room with an Olympic feel and used some other props. We even sang the Australian National Anthem when we gave out the medals in the end. It was fun, made us laugh and people remembered those moments.

Recently, in the last retreat, we had the *Survivor* theme (as in the USA's reality TV show that has been running now for over 35 seasons). We decided prior to retreat to order the custom-made headscarfs in two colours which meant we would have two tribes: we had the Nat and Stu tribe (red and blue). Each tribe ended up being 10 people exactly and we played all sorts of book-related games over the full weekend. At the end one tribe won. It was a nice state breaker and the games were quick so they didn't take away from the work we were seriously doing. It bonded the teams and there was a healthy level of competition throughout the weekend.

Social Time

Make sure you schedule in some fun and social time. Mealtimes are usually dedicated for this but you can bring in some structure to it at other times. We make night two our fun fancy dress night where we all come out looking dressed up in the weekend theme. It gets people to step into being a different character; we arrange stand-up drinks, cocktail style, before we sit down to dinner and we take lots of photos for our memories. As we are away, no one feels shy to dress up (there may always be one that won't, but most people love doing something different if you frame it right).

Make sure you take lots of photos and you do one of a group shot. We live stream on social media too during this time and others express interest in being there at the next retreat—more hot leads!

After dinner we usually like to retreat to a sitting area or back to our training room where we can have a dance or a few more drinks in a more informal way. So much fun and laughs happen and this bonds the group even stronger. When people are leaving only 48 hours later, it's like they are leaving their best friends, not strangers they only met two days ago.

Workbook With Handouts

I know it may seem obvious that you would have a workbook, but I didn't at my first retreat. Would you believe I used to hand out separate pieces of paper for each thing that we were doing? Then someone said to me, why don't you give these in a display folder or even better, print everything you give and make a bound workbook. Easy as that and makes you more professional.

I used to do it in the display books first and do my own printing at home, but now I just tell my printer what I need and how many and then they get picked up a few days later—even easier!

I like to print sticky labels with people's names and the date of their retreat so it's nicely personalised and put it on their desk when they arrive in the training room.

The Run Sheet

In the previous chapter I shared some of our timings throughout the retreat in the crew instructions. At the beginning of your workbook of handouts, I suggest that you put a run sheet for every participant to have for themselves. Ours is quite detailed and scheduled to the very last minute, so I ensure everyone, including myself, stays on track with it.

Test and measure what works best and adjust it as you see how it all feels.

Wow, that is a lot of ideas to now think of and get ready to action for your retreat. So what are you waiting for? Get to work!

Chapter 8
Your Customer's Journey

It is only when I started writing this book that I realised how much I actually do to make my retreats happen. How many intricate details get put into action and thought about to make it all a reality. In an earlier chapter, I shared the logistics around the half-day workshop and now it's time to take you on a tour of the Customer Journey system. Here I want you to start thinking about what happens with my client from the moment they commit to working with me to the moment that they are finished and beyond. There are seven main stages:

1. Onboarding
2. Preparation
3. Lead-up
4. Pre-retreat
5. At retreat
6. Post-retreat
7. The future

Onboarding

You just made a sale! Yes yes yes—it's super exciting. You get the privilege of helping a person transform and get new results in their life and business. But first, you must ensure you onboard them properly. We have a template in Asana (the project management program) that has a number of steps that need to be completed either by me, my husband or our assistant. Here is a sample list:

- signed agreement filed away
- payment completed for deposit and direct deposits set up if on payment plan
- introduced new author into the secret groups
- send new author their welcome postcard from Send Out Cards
- initiate new author sequence of emails that give them an orientation of all they get and where to get it
- email sent to author to book in their prep session.

Once those have been completed we can delete that project around the author's onboarding.

Preparation

As you noticed in the previous section we have an email that goes out with a link so that the author can book themselves for their prep session. Even though our clients have retreats that may be nine to twelve months away, the prep session is one that calms their nerves, gives them direction and focus, and establishes that the decision they have made is the right one.

You want your clients to feel like they have begun their journey to transformation. For those that are not coming to their retreat for a while, we touch base again with them at one month prior to retreat. In fact, we touch base with everyone one month prior to retreat to see what may have changed around their books and what further support they may need.

Over time we have also developed a detailed 20-page mini manual prior to meeting for the session that guides the author through what will happen at our one-to-one and gives them details that pretty much answer most questions. You may not start with one of those, but you will notice as you repeat yourself over and over that you can document that for your clients to digest for themselves.

Lead-Up

As there may be quite some time before your new clients come to their retreat program, think about how you can keep them engaged in the community and with the information they can access in the meantime. Here are some ideas:

- monthly webinar support call
- online community where they can be around like-minded people
- other workshops they can get access to before coming to retreat (for example, we run 3 x year two-day masterclasses face to face that our authors can attend as part of their program)
- email sequence with short interesting videos they can receive on auto pilot.

Bottom line is, stay in touch, be top of mind with them and keep getting them excited about what is coming up.

Pre-Retreat System

The best time to initiate a pre-retreat system is one month before the retreat. If my retreat is 15 – 17 May then on April 15 I initiate this system. Again, this is something we have set up in Asana to manage and tick off consistently so that nothing slips through the cracks or gets forgotten.

Here is an example of tasks that get completed in the last month:

- send out the one-month email with Mindset Webinar link

- confirm venue with numbers
- set up our logistics webinar that happens 10 days before retreat
- host the logistics webinar 10 days before retreat
- check we have all printed products we need
- start a secret Facebook Messenger message one month out with all that are attending this retreat
- get name tags, release forms and any other printed collateral ready
- confirm who is doing transfers and crewing
- buy extra snacks, potatoes and candles for the exercises.

These all end up being dated and assigned to whoever is responsible for each task. That way nothing slips through our fingers and all communication is consistent.

At Retreat

You may like to refer to the crew instructions sheet I shared earlier for a detailed run-through of the system during retreat.

Post-Retreat

Part of our Asana template includes all the tasks that need to occur post-retreat to close off the event and everything we have promised. Here is a sample list of what those tasks may be:

- Give all participants access to our secret Dropbox.
- Put all the photos and videos from the retreat in our Dropbox.
- Send a postcard with our group photo post-retreat via Send Out Cards.

- Initiate the post-retreat sequence of accountability emails.
- Send any other promised resources via the post-retreat email the day after retreat.
- Pay out any affiliates.
- Edit and upload all testimonials on YouTube.
- Call all authors 7 – 10 days after the retreat.

Again, these are allocated to either myself, my husband or our assistant. Once done we can delete that project and finalise the event as fully followed up.

The Future

Once you have finalised the retreat, we manage any future questions, emails and conversations as they arise. We have a system in place for online and offline accountability to ensure our authors follow through to completion. Now that we have the set-up of our own publishing company, we will have extra systems to manage the publishing process which we used to outsource fully to another business.

Remember, once the systems are in place, you can remove all the clutter from your mind and focus on just the tasks for that day. Once you can outsource most of your tasks, life becomes easy and all you need to do is focus on doing what you love doing best. It doesn't get any better than that.

It's time now to start writing some initial processes for your retreat. How will your customer journey unfold? Maybe you will have similar systems or bring something completely new and unique into the mix. Have fun!

Chapter 9
Value Adding Secrets

Giving your clients things they never expected they would get from you takes the value of their experience through your retreat program to the next level. There is Wow Factor and then there is double Wow Factor. Here I will give you some examples of extra bonuses you can give your clients that will surprise and delight them. Here is the list and an explanation in detail of what it all means:

- a secret Dropbox full of resources and goodies for success
- guest experts they didn't know were coming
- extra products they were not expecting to receive
- IT help
- future workshops they can participate in to stay connected in the community and keep learning.

The Secret Dropbox

Dropbox is a file storage system on the cloud that you can use to share documents with anyone. It also keeps all your files safe rather than just having them only on your computer or laptop. You can access your Dropbox from any computer or mobile device. If you don't store your files on the cloud, please don't risk it and buy yourself an annual subscription to Dropbox which gives you 1TB of storage (which is massive, by the way) for around $120USD.

There is 2GB of storage as a free entry into Dropbox if you want to check it out. So what I do for my authors is I have set up a dedicated Dropbox with all systems, resources, PowerPoints and links to video footage they can access for life. That's right, for life! I add more cool stuff and update the documents in that Dropbox regularly as I grow and learn new stuff. I give access to the authors during their retreat and they really respond with an astounded look on their faces, some of them even making comments like '... and we get all of that too?'

Please make sure if you set this up that you give your clients view rights only not editing rights, as if you allow them to edit they could be accidentally changing the files for everybody. They can certainly cut and paste files from that Dropbox on their computer and then do any editing they like.

Guest Experts

Who does something your clients need and complements you but is not in competition with you? Think about potential collaborative partners. I collaborate with the Publicity Princess—Kate Engler—who does a Meet the Media program and with the Meet Up Queen—Francesca Moi—who teaches people to build a following and get bums on seats. They are both a complement and someone my authors would benefit learning from but they are in no way in competition with what I offer. Vice versa, their clients would benefit from what I do, thus it's a match made in heaven.

Kate and Francesca have come to my retreats on numerous occasions to deliver a teach segment to my authors and have made me look even better in front of my clients.

Whomever you decide to put in front of your clients, make sure you check them out and see them speak first before you bring them in front of your high-end clients. They must make you look great and your clients receive massive value from them. This also gives you a bit of a break in presenting while at the same time you become the hero and surprise your clients with this bonus.

Tangible Products Rule

I spoke at length about tangibles and intangibles in the first chapter. It is time to revisit them. Having something to take away as a memento or materials after a retreat really adds another level of value to your clients. People love the Dropbox but it's not something they can touch and feel. I like to give them a few books, a product generator manual and maybe some themed stuff (like the headscarves for the *Survivor* theme) to take home with them after the retreat.

Ensure that you tell people to allow extra space in their luggage for a couple of kilos, depending on what you are giving them to take home. Our participants are mostly getting to us by flying in so we must tell them they will be taking home extra bits and pieces. Even so, they don't know what, so they are still surprised when they get them at the start of retreat.

IT Help

I have been blessed to have had a previous author who is an IT expert (that is his business—check out Right Click IT and ask for James Bomford). He also loves coming back to retreat to crew. He has been at more than 10 retreats since the time he wrote his book *What the F#$% is the Cloud?* When we have him on board it really takes away the IT questions from us as mentors and we can handle the other bits we need to be helping with. IT is in everything nowadays. If you don't get good at it, you will get left behind. Really make it a priority to learn as much as you can—it will save you so much time and frustration.

Who do you know that is great at IT? They don't need to have a company or business in IT like James does, but I am sure you know a few people that you would call tech savvy. See if you can take them along as crew at your retreat. You will be so glad when you can divert those questions to a person like that so you can focus on what you do best.

Future Workshops

I don't know about you but it's been said it's harder to find a new client than to sell to those that are already working with you. Beyond your retreat, your clients may want more time with you, to learn some aspects of what you have been teaching them deeper or they may want some more handholding one-on-one.

There are two ways you can look at this value: you either keep giving awesome training for free or you can have a next step offer. We offer 3 x two-day masterclasses our authors can attend for life to learn the marketing and leveraging skills in depth beyond bringing out their books. There is no further upsell, but at the two-day masterclasses they may buy my planners or books or even bring along a buddy that is not our client as a referral.

The thinking here is that by continuing to connect with your high-end clients you continue to deepen the relationship and rapport between you. You are more likely to stay top of mind with them and they are more likely to continue being raving fans that continue referring new business to you. It's all about the relationships and how you nurture them.

It's your turn now—what do the above look like for you?

How can you get organised and make everyone's life a lot easier when they don't have you by their side every single day? Document your ideas and then make them happen.

Chapter 10
Outsourcing Smarts

Running any type of events, especially retreats, requires a lot of planning, admin work and co-ordination to execute in a way that your clients will be delighted. In the beginning, you may be able to do this independently, but as you grow, you will need to consider getting help, at the very least around the administrative side of things. Ultimately the goal should be that you become the maestro to the people that are doing different parts of your business and you just focus on delivery. By the way, delivery can be outsourced too.

The below advice on outsourcing can be used for any type of freelancer or team member you may need. Outsourcing can occur in two ways: offline help like delivery, physical team members that work in the business, or online whereby you hire experts purely online as their work can be completed through the power of the internet. For example, graphic design, editing, copywriting, website design, printing on demand, etc.

The key to outsourcing is that you have people that will understand your business values and business so that you end up with a smooth system whereby your clients are treated in the same way as you would treat them. Sometimes business owners don't want to lose control of what they know they can do best, but this is to the detriment of that business owner.

With systemisation and early handholding of your team members, you will be able to train them up to a level you are proud of.

With the onset of online outsourcing, we can now achieve outcomes in our businesses a lot easier and at a cheaper price point. Take my virtual assistant, for an example. She is based in the Philippines and as the socio economic status there is a lot lower, what I pay her for a full-time wage is a great rate for where she lives and it's an amazing rate for me to have her as it would cost me five times more here. I used to think that I didn't know what I could give a virtual assistant and held off on getting one for two years too long. I kept thinking that I would get one once I wrote up more of my systems. That never happened. One day I took the leap with only one system written and started her on that. In the two weeks that she was completing that one task, I thought of more things I could get her to do and since then I keep building more systems and tasks she can help me with. She is now an invaluable part of our team and lives. She is super loyal and has been with us for three years full time.

So how do you find yourself online experts to help you with your business operations and sometimes delivery of what you have promised your clients? There are two places: Fiverr and Upwork. Fiverr is great for cheap and fast small jobs and most things are $5 on there. I have discovered some great people through Fiverr. Upwork you can use to find more long-term freelancers, virtual assistants and higher-quality people. This is where you can post a job to look for whom you need. If you do end up getting a virtual assistant, I recommend you use Asana for the project management of what will be required of them and by when. Once you trust your person, you may consider working with them privately without the middle person being Fiverr or Upwork as they do take sometimes up to 25% of the freelancer's fees you pay them. I pay my assistant now directly through PayPal and in a way it's like a pay rise for her.

So how do you choose? You will be inundated with sometimes 30–40 job applications and this can lead to overwhelm. I always start at the top of who is the best match recommended and go through the applications. Things I look for before I decide to speak to someone are: where they are located as time zoning is important to me; how much care they have taken in applying for the job; whether they have a good job success rate through Upwork; how much they have earned through Upwork (as if they have a 100% job success rate but only earned $200 it is not that accurate of how good they are); and if they have sent a portfolio I look through it to see if I like what I see (this is only relevant to visual style jobs).

If I am happy with all of the above, I shortlist the person and send them a private message to ask more questions from them and see how well and quickly they communicate and respond. To me one of my highest values is speed so I love working with those that get back to me within a day, if not sooner. If it's someone I am planning to have as part of my team, I ask to do a video chat with them via the platform. Video is powerful so you can check how good their internet is, how you feel about them in terms of the way they speak, their surroundings of where they work and just a general gut feeling on who they are as a person. If I like them, I will ask them to quote me on specific things I am looking for and then I wait to see how quickly they respond with that quote. Another super important step to watch out for.

When you do a video interview, these are some general questions you should ask and discuss:

- Thank them for their time to meet you and their willingness to do video.
- Ask them about their experience, length of time in business, and their day-to-day life and activities

(this can tell a lot about their availability and current responsibilities).

- Tell them a bit about your background, story, passion and needs.
- Talk about your business values and how you like things from the start.
- Establish turnaround times and back-up plans should anything change.
- Ask them for a quote if you like them and tell them when you will get back to them with your answer.

If you are happy with everything and would like to work with them, I suggest the first few times you use them go through the Upwork system as it keeps you safe. You are protected in case you are not happy or something odd happens. Your payment gets held in what they call the 'escrow' and only once you are happy with your work they release the payment to the freelancer. Once you feel you trust them, you may like to pay them privately 50% on start of a project and 50% on completion.

If you are working with someone full time or part time continuously, get them to keep a time sheet as it's very hard to monitor this remotely. Once you trust someone, you don't need to be micromanaging them and you can let them be independent.

Outsourcing will allow you to breathe a sigh of relief. You will wonder how the hell you did everything yourself. Don't delay it as your business won't be able to grow and scale without the help of a bigger team.

Now think of something you have been putting off and jump on Upwork to hire someone to help you with it. Get that first taste of what it feels like and then you will be empowered to do more of it as you build your confidence in outsourcing.

Chapter 11
Get People Talking

The hardest part of launching your retreat program is now behind you. You may have already run your retreat and want to do more and more and more. Well, I am sorry to say, the marketing and sales does not stop. In fact, 90% of your time you will be investing in content marketing, meeting new people, delivering workshops offline, webinars online and so on ... 10% of your time will be servicing your clients through your system. Once you have a tribe of happy clients, why not use the super power of word of mouth to get a few easier sales into your future retreats? Usually when a happy client refers someone on to you, they have done most of the selling for you. It's up to you to complete the conversion and get started with that new client. The only thing is that most business owners don't know how to ask others to refer to them. I have come to understand that you need to train your clients how to refer to you. I do this on the last day of my retreat for around 10 minutes in one of the segments called 'Future Opportunities'.

The first thing you also should decide is if you will incentivise referrals. I call it the Kickback Affiliate incentive. We give $500 cash to our referrer upon the completion of the author's retreat. Do not pay this out immediately as I have learnt the hard way where people have cancelled or delayed their retreat to later on. Only upon completion of their program should the incentive be paid out. Also, don't delay any further paying out the incentive if you want more referrals. I have a task on the Monday after my retreat to fulfil that promise to my client referral. I have honoured this affiliate kickback more than 30 times so far, which is thousands of saved dollars for me in paid advertising.

There may be a bit of a grey area about these types of referrals I want to make you aware of. Sometimes people may see their friend on social media and enquire with you or you may have met them and years later they become a client already having a connection with one of your authors. What I consider a proper referral is when people have come from the below strategies and there has not been a lag time in them becoming a client. There has to be some kind of honour system here at play, but so long as you keep the lines of communication open and you explain properly what happened then everyone will be fine.

One particular situation that arose recently was that two of my authors knew the new author I signed up. One author lived in Perth and the other in Brisbane. The Brisbane author, however, referred the new author to my Brisbane half-day workshop and she signed up straight after the event. A month later I was catching up with my Perth author and she discussed how she knew the new author and they had been friends. She asked if she qualified for the kickback incentive. I was honest and clearly explained that the new author was directly referred to the half day which was where the conversion occurred, thus qualifying the author from Brisbane.

So here are the things that are included in my training on how I explain to my clients to refer to me. I also give them a piece of paper that has the following and I explain in order of how I recommend they prioritise what to say to the potential new author:

1. Tell people about our awesome half-day workshop— get them to buy a standard <u>ticket here</u>. We will then upgrade them to a VIP ticket on the day.
2. Refer people into a <u>FREE Webinar</u>. They will progress to a call which is where we will speak to them about retreat.
3. Ask for permission for us to call them—not the other way around. The best introductions are via a three-way Facebook message. We will in most cases invite them first to the half-day workshop.

I also explain the worst way to refer to us is to give someone else our business card or website. Most people will think it's a great idea at the time but won't take any action with that information.

So, what does this look like for your retreat business? It's important to think about and not miss out on the opportunity of your biggest raving fans to refer to you. They are the best referrers, usually immediately after their experience. Ensure that you also tweak and adjust how you communicate referring to you. You will find better ways that give you even better results.

The Power of Collaboration

The next step is to start thinking about your collaborative partners. We spoke earlier about having some of them come and present during your retreat to add more value. In these cases if they have an offer you can become their affiliate kickback person, especially if you are more likely to refer to them over them to you. It can happen that way sometimes because of the nature of businesses.

With some collaborations money does not need to cross hands; with others where it may be more one-sided then a kickback would be a great incentive to work towards. Only do this with those you trust and know will provide an amazing service to your clients. I've a bit of both. It's great to extra passive cash flow and makes for a great value add to my clients. It also helps my collaborative partner which is where we strengthen our relationship.

The power of a network and strong relationships is the backbone to any thriving business. Ensure you continue investing your time to get to know people and help them. You never know when you will need to ask for help. For example, when my Facebook ads were going through a really tough time and bums on seats became an issue, I reached out to my network and collaborative partners and together we did all we could to get me those bums on seats. That six-month period ended up being just as good as any time of the year and our sales didn't suffer as a result of it. I always want people to learn the basics of _Bums on Seats_ before diving into the world of paid advertising. When you know the basics and foundational stuff you can always fall back on it should anything go wrong or slow down with the paid advertising.

Is it time to design your 'Get them Talking' system and plan when you will train your clients during the retreat in it? Then make a list of your collaborative partners and if you don't have any, who would you like to meet that can become one?

Chapter 12
Going National and International

So you want to go global? Congratulations ... Arriving at a point in your business where you are ready to take that next step is exciting and a bit nerve-racking. Just trust that you will know when the time is right to do this. Usually once you have run your retreats for a few years successfully and you are in need for a new stretch and challenge, you will want to step up and explore this possibility. But why? There are many reasons why you may want to go global and these can include:
- new challenge
- expand the business in other countries with a greater population
- establish a new network in a new country
- make more money
- great publicity for your business and brand back home.

Sometimes you may think you are going for one of the above reasons and then after the fact realise the outcome was something completely unexpected. One thing I'd like to say about this is no matter what, you will learn something. The benefits will be clear when you look back on that experience. I can guarantee you the experience will enrich you and make you more resilient.

Before I speak about the awesome benefits, here are some hard realities to expect when you embark on this journey:

1. The legal implications of running your business in another country—you must research, ask lots of questions and figure out if this is a possibility for you. Some countries are harder to establish your business into and others are easier. For example, in the UAE I have a partner that is taking care of all the legal aspects of our venture there, in the USA I had a sponsor and in NZ I didn't need anyone as it's considered almost like Australia. Take time to understand this as the worst thing that can happen is you spend money on marketing and set-up and then you cannot enter the country for business purposes.

2. Marketing costs—expect these can double or triple. You will be entering a cold market that has never heard from you. You will need to build an audience and advertise perhaps for double the period you do at home. Please note that in Australia there is an export grant called the EDMG you may be eligible to apply for. We did and we got 50% of our marketing cost reimbursed. This is available for up to eight years of international work and you can bundle up your first two years as one year. Remember that as with every application there is a $5000 admin fee they apply to your application. If you bundle the first two years you will be saving $5000.

3. Travel time and cost considerations—depending on where you live, you must consider the cost and time of travel to your new destinations. National travel is quite easy, international can be more of a challenge, especially if you live in countries such as myself—Australia or New Zealand. Most international travel is long haul and this takes more time and money to

make a reality, let alone your energy. This is one of the reasons I ran my business internationally for two years and now decide to remain Australia-centric as it was taking too much time and effort to be travelling long distances for the business. I still love going international, but nowadays that is reserved for pleasure not business.

4. Cultural considerations—stepping into another country, even one that speaks the same language as you, will see you hit some cultural challenges and differences that you will need to learn how to navigate. These can be frustrating, surprising and sometimes pleasing. As we know there is good and not so good in every culture. Be prepared for these—read up on a specific culture and observe what happens where possible. Nothing beats you being there and experiencing it in real time. You will pick up and adjust as you go along. This is very interesting yet super stressful at the time. Trust me, you will laugh later on about all the things that stressed you out.

I am really glad I did go international for two years. I grew as a person, I learnt about new cultures and how they make decisions, operate and are as clients. I made a ton of new friends, partners, collaborators and established a network of raving fans. I have lots of people I can go back and visit in the future. I've said it before and I will say it again—nothing beats that face-to-face contact you have when you make the effort to go and meet people on their playground. They appreciate the effort, they build a stronger relationship with you and remember you for a long time as you are a bit different.

My business perception back home grew to now being an international brand with clients from over 20 countries. I use this credibility to show potential new clients that we commit to a process and execute on our commitments. Credibility is built when people can see you follow through, you do what you say and you are visible consistently in your space. That's why writing a book is one of the best ways to build credibility. People can see you have put in the effort, committed to a process that scared everyone and that you back your knowledge and message. They know that if someone has gone as far as writing a book about their expertise, they must be serious about their business and helping people.

The last thing I would like to share about going international is to consider having a partnership with someone that is on the ground in the other country, already has an established network and is willing to promote you. You may not know anyone like that, but once you put the intention out there you may find that you attract someone like that in your life. Having my partner Moustafa Hamwi in the UAE has made that venture very successful and profitable for both of us. There were definitely times when I wanted to give up, but I have learnt that you must persist through the early teething stages and getting used to each other's working styles before you reach cruising altitude and start working like a well-oiled machine.

To your Global Domination!!! Go forth and conquer ...

Final Words

The only thing that awaits now is for you to take action and get onto planning your first retreat. Read through this book a few times and implement the steps I have suggested. It takes some time to build up your own infrastructure around this.

You are also invited to join me in a couple of Facebook groups that I have: Ultimate Business Support and Author Your Way to Riches.

I wish you the best of success with your retreat adventures. Take lots of photos and share those with the rest of us.

Finally—PLEASE ... :) if you enjoyed this book, it would be AWESOME if you could leave a quick review on Amazon RIGHT HERE.

It's really quick and it would mean the WORLD!!! Thank you so very much—YOU ARE THE BEST!!!

Happy retreating and all the very best!

Natasa Denman
NatasaDenman.com #ultimate48hourauthor

Did you enjoy the book?

... then it would be super-duper awesome if you could <u>leave a review on Amazon</u> and share the joy :) (or whatever else you would like to share)

This also helps interested readers to work out if the book will be helpful for them.

You extra help is enormously appreciated and <u>you can post your review here</u>.

More Natasa Denman Books

Click on any of the book images and you will taken to the purchase page on Amazon. Alternatively, you can visit www.writeabook.com.au to check out all of Natasa Denman's books and products.

The 7 Ultimate Secrets to Weight Loss

Ninja Couch Marketing

Bums on Seats

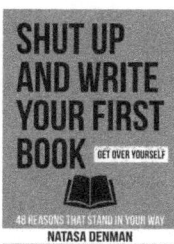

Shut Up and Write Your First Book

Guilt Free Parents

Natasa Denman reveals ...
1000 Days to a Million Dollar
Coaching Business from
Home

Ultimate 48 Hour Author

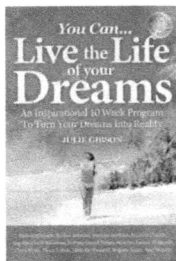

You Can Live the Life of your
Dreams

About the Author

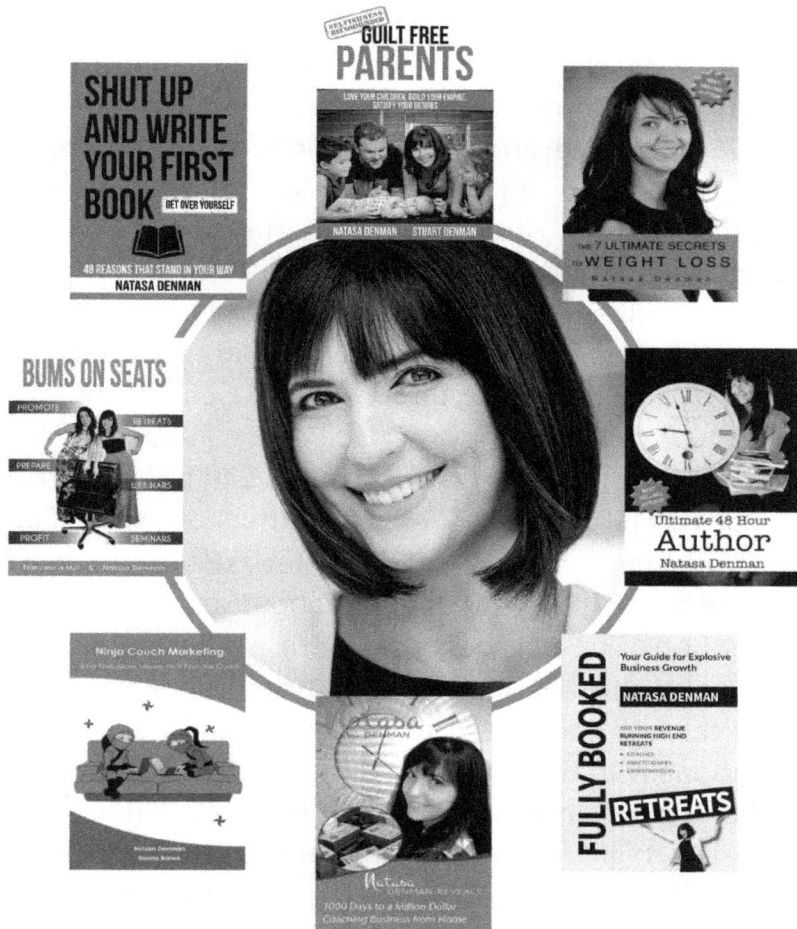

Natasa Denman was born and raised in Skopje, Macedonia up to the age of 14, after which she emigrated to Melbourne, Australia to be with her mum. They were separated for two and a half years. She didn't speak English and found it challenging in the first two years to fit into the new country and culture. Her zest for learning and achievement fast tracked this process and she had high performance results in her academic endeavours.

Natasa has a Bachelor of Applied Science (Psychology/ Psychophysiology), Diploma in Life Coaching, NLP Practitioner Certification, Practitioner of Matrix Therapies, holds a Black Belt in Taekwondo and is a Professional Certified Coach (PCC) through the International Coaching Federation.

Being creative and writing books is something she never planned to do. Her passion for business and marketing was the reason she wrote her first book *The 7 Ultimate Secrets to Weight Loss* in June 2011. This book put her first business on the map and enabled her husband to join her full time in the business a year later. She has also written *Ultimate 48 Hour Author, Natasa Denman Reveals ... 1000 Days to a Million Dollar Coaching Business from Home,* is a contributor of *You Can ... Live the Life of Your Dreams* and *Speaking Successfully,* a co-author of *Ninja Couch Marketing, Bums on Seats* and *Guilt Free Parents.*

Ultimate 48 Hour Author came about as a result of the success books have brought to Natasa's business. Aside from books she has also written five programs and has three licensed systems that are being utilised by others internationally in their businesses.

She is now known as The Ultimate 48 Hour Author. Natasa is a highly sought after professional speaker (CSP accredited) and Australia's leading authority on helping first-time authors publish their books. She has helped over 250 solopreneurs become first-time published authors in just four years in Australia, USA, New Zealand and UAE. She also has clients from 10 other international countries.

In eight short years in business, Natasa has been nominated for The Telstra Businesswoman of the Year twice and was a finalist in AusMumpreneur of the Year in Product Innovation.

Appearing in all major media outlets across Australia including *the Sydney Morning Herald*, the *Financial Review* and *The Age*, Natasa is changing the way people do business in Australia and the world. She now runs a seven-figure business with her husband and three children, travelling the world, spreading her message and helping small businesses thrive. This year Natasa's mum also joined the business.

The Denman family's passion is to continue to build this as a fully fledged family business helping thousands around the world become first-time authors without compromising on also living a balanced lifestyle. Their motto is Work Hard – Play Hard, whereby they work intensely for five and half months in the year, spend two and a half months on building new systems and value to what they do, and they travel and holiday four months of the year.

This is what they want to enable others to create when building their own entrepreneurial ventures with the help of a published book.

Ultimate 48 Hour Author lives by Four Values: Fun, Fast, Fame and above all FAMILY.

Natasa's websites:
www.natasadenman.com
www.ultimate48hourauthor.com.au

Email: natasa@natasadenman.com

www.ingramcontent.com/pod-product-compliance
Lightning Source LLC
Chambersburg PA
CBHW031903200326
41597CB00012B/521